Echoes of JUSTICE

**Editor
Ayşegül Gönül**

EDITOR

AYŞEGÜL GÖNÜL

DESIGN AND ILLUSTRATIONS

MUHSIN NAZIF

ADVOCATES OF SILENCED TURKEY

AST is a 501(c)(3) tax exempt, not for profit charitable and educational organization based in New Jersey, USA exclusively for defending human and civil rights.

ISBN: 9798328142724

CONTACT

271 US 46, #F 203 Fairfield, NJ, 07004
help@silencedturkey.org

WEB & SOCIAL MEDIA

www.silencedturkey.org
@silencedturkey
facebook.com/silencedturkey
youtube.com/advocatesofsilencedturkey

Those Who Contributed to the Kahoot Competition and Book Study

Ayşegül Gönül
Editor and Competition Coordinator

Kubra Ünver
Presenter

Kemal Karanfil
Question Preparation

Adem Yavuz Arslan
Question Preparation

Sümeyra Korkut
Translation

Ahmet Kaval
Translation

Dilara Guzel
Question Preparation

Eyup Esen
Question Preparation

Dr.Kari O'Rourke
Question Preparation

Dr. Doğan Yüceloğlu
Question Preparation

Dulat Bekbolsynor
Question Preparation

Fatih Canlı
Flyer Preparation

Fatih Yanık
Technical Support

Hasan Gönül
Question Preparation and Translation

Hasan Erdem
Technical Support

Judge Kemal Karanfil
Question Preparation

Mercan Kuloğlu
Translation

Meryem Yağlıdere
Translation

Özgür Yağlıdere
Technical Support

Özlem Kara
Question Preparation

Büşra Saraçoğlu
Question Preparation

Zülal Gönül
Translation

Enes Korkut
Technical Support

Adem Özel
Question Preparation

Nese Muhsinoglu
Translation

Nuran Erdoğan
Translation

Nefise Nihal Gönül
Translation

Enes Korkut
Technical Support

CONTENTS

ADVOCATES OF SILENCED TURKEY

AST is a 501(c)(3) Not for Profit charitable and educational organization based in NJ, exclusively for defending human and civil rights.

Our aim is, address all forms of human rights violations being perpetrated in Turkey-- including civil, political, economic, social and cultural-- based on the tenets upheld in fundamental human rights documents;

To speak up against any forms of genocide, crimes against humanity, arbitrary detentions, cases of torture and ill treatment, and discrimination, and stand up for principles and values such as the right to life, the rule of law, the right to privacy, freedom of expression, freedom of thought, conscience and religion, and freedom of associations;

To utilize all human rights advocacy tools, mechanisms, and systems that can possibly be utilized in order to protect and demand the fundamental human rights of those whose voices are being silenced in Turkey and beyond;

And to hold accountable the perpetrators who are denying individuals in Turkey and beyond their fundamental Human Rights while providing the victims with the opportunity to obtain justice and reparation.

Introduction

The Kahoot competitions we organize every month to raise awareness among young people about human rights violations worldwide and in Turkey have reached over 10,000 views on YouTube globally. The impact of these competitions on young people and the feedback we receive have been a great source of motivation for us. Among the feedback we receive from young people, there are expressions like "thank you for presenting to us the incidents that happen without discrimination in a language that young people can understand and enjoy, which is Kahoot competitions." These feedbacks have been a great source of satisfaction and guidance for us.

We are delighted to observe that young people gain significant motivation in preparing for the future by learning about human rights violations worldwide through these competitions. Additionally, seeing our guests share the lessons they have learned from their own experiences of ongoing human rights violations has also contributed greatly to our followers' awareness. The motivating effect of the prizes we send to the top three winners of the competition is also crucial. Seeing that these prizes motivate the winners and increase interest in our competitions brings us great joy.

We realized that the success of our competitions has led us to consider recording all the competition questions and the valuable thoughts of our guests and turning them into a book. In this regard, we have completed our book with a great team effort and we are very happy to make this book available to young people and all volunteers who are sensitive to human rights. We hope that our book will be found in every home and that it will inspire the future golden generation to strive for a better world by learning from the lessons of human rights violations. We would like to thank everyone who has supported us on this journey.

1 Which is a condition of the Great Charter of Freedoms, signed between King John the Homeless and the barons in England?
a) Magna Carta Libertatum
b) Petition of Rights
c) Bill of Rights
d) Habeas Corpus

2 Which organization is within the body of the European Convention on Human Rights?
a) League of Nations
b) United Nations
c) Council of Europe
d) European Commission

3 Who was it that rejected the notion that Blacks should give up their seats on the bus and sparked the civil rights movement in the US?
a) Rosa Parks
b) Muhammad Ali
c) Malcom X
d) Benjamin Franklin

4 Who is Nadia Murad?
a) An activist seeking educational equality for girls
b) A politician seeking religious equality for Yazidis in Iraq
c) Nobel Peace Prize owner, who fought against sexual violence
d) A prominent LGBT activist in Iraq

5 Who is a socialist Human Rights activist in Turkey, practices a different religion than the majority, but stands by all kinds of victims without discrimination?
a) Azra Akin
b) Huda Kaya
c) Natali Avazyan
d) Melek Cetinkaya

6 What is considered the most important human right in America?
a) The right to take up arms
b) Freedom of speech
c) Freedom of religion

7 Who is the teacher who died in custody on July 15, wanted to be buried in the grave of traitors and was reinstated after 1.5 years in Turkey?
a) Esma Uludag
b) Halime Gulsu
c) Gökhan Açıkkollu
d) Ugur Abdurrezzak

8 Who is the deputy who is the voice of the people with the decree laws, who voiced their grievances in the Parliament, on YouTube, and who went to jail?
a) Sezgin Tanrikulu
b) Hüda Kaya
c) Omer Faruk Gergerlioglu
d) Veli Saçılık

9 Who is the famous NBA player, as a family were victims of July 15, and who voiced this injustice on every platform?
a) Ersan Ilyasova
b) Enes Kanter
c) Burak Yilmaz
d) Hedayet Turk

10 Nelson Mandela is the leader of the civil, peaceful resistance against the British occupation in India.
a) True
b) False

Did You Know That?

Hilmi Sezgin 1st Kahoot competition 1st place

Hello everyone, those who are my age and feel young. Welcome to AST's kahoot program. I'm Hilmi, greetings from Europe. Like the young audience, I also participated in AST's kahoot competition and came in first place. I saw this competition from AST's announcement on its Twitter account. I immediately joined the competition and came first. You can also participate in the competition and invite your friends to this competition. Who knows, maybe you'll come first.

Mahatma Gandhi

Did you know that Gandhi, who is still considered a hero with his unarmed struggle in India, was actually imprisoned for seven years with four arrest warrants?

Between 1922 and 1942, he was in prison for seven years. Why? Because he had four arrest warrants for him and was an unarmed human rights defender.

Human Rights Day

Did you know that Human Rights Day is observed internationally on 10th of December?

Human Rights Day is celebrated across the world on 10th of December every year. The date was adopted in 1948 by the United Nations General Assembly, when the Universal Declaration of Human Rights was approved.

11. It is a convention that includes the prevention of all forms of violence against women and the punishment of criminals.
a) Ankara Convention
b) Izmir Convention
c) Diyarbakir Convention
d) Istanbul Convention

12. The first political-legal document in the history of Islam, which foresees living together, prepared with the participation of different religious and ethnic groups.
a) Taif Agreement
b) Mecca Convention
c) Certificate of Medina
d) Hudaybiyah Agreement

13. How much is the application fee to the ECTHR (European Court of Human Rights)?
a) It is free
b) 20 Euros
c) 15 pounds
d) $20

14. What is the name of the Photo Contest organized by AST to announce human rights and violations and to be a voice for the oppressed?
a) 15 July Photo Contest
b) Kara Efe Photo Contest
c) Hope Photo Contest
d) Broken Hearts Photo Contest

15. Who is the researcher, writer and Islamic scholar who was sentenced to 19 years and 2 months for his column in Zaman?
a) Ahmet Altan
b) Mehmet Altan
c) Ilhan Isbilen
d) Ali Unal

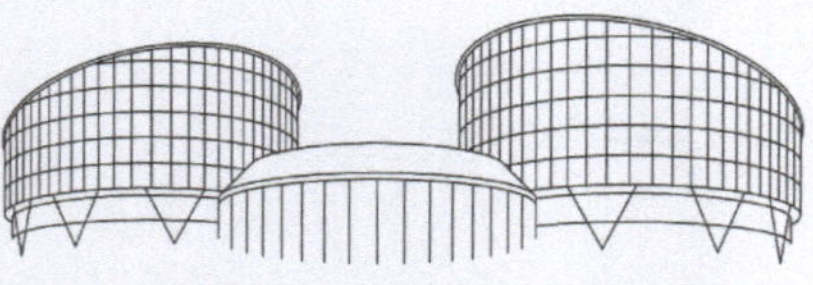

16. What is the most common human rights violation worldwide today?
a) The crime of torture of political prisoners
b) Discrimination against indigenous people
c) Violence against women and girls
d) Forced child labor

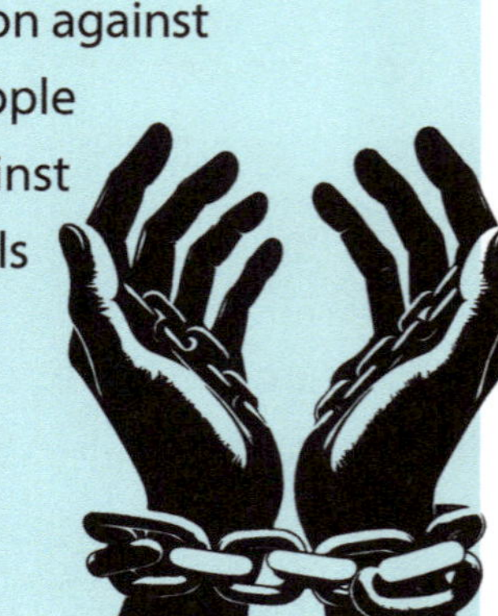

17 According to the 2019 report of the International Labor Organization, ___ is working as child workers.
a) 82 million
b) 102 million
c) 202 million
d) 152 million

18 According to the Universal Declaration of Human Rights, which of the following rights protects individuals from discrimination based on race, color, sex, language, religion, political or other opinion, national or social origin, property, birth, or other status?
a) Right to child labor
b) Right to freedom of expression
c) Right to equal pay for equal work
d) Right to forced marriage

19 According to the Human Rights Reports, how many Turkish citizens were abducted in and out of Turkey after 2016?
a) 100
b) 144
c) 57
d) 256

20 What is the name of the program that AST encourages young people to write?
a) A story of hope from 2000 refugee children
b) Poetry competition in memory of Hatice Akçabay
c) Human Rights Painting Contest

Did You Know That?

Susan B. Anthony

Did you know that an American civil rights activist was arrested for voting illegally?

There was a time where there was a brave American civil rights activist who voted in a presidential election. At that time women were not allowed to vote. 2 weeks later she was arrested and eventually fined 100 dollars for voting illegally.
Her name was Susan B. Anthony.

Mother Teresa

Did you know that social service volunteer and human rights activist Mother Teresa received

the Nobel Peace Prize in 1979 for her charitable activities?

Mother Teresa, whose birth name was Agnes Gonca Boyaci, was born in Skopje in 1910. She was of Albanian origin. During a visit to Skopje in 1980, when she was asked whether she was an Albanian, a Macedonian or a Serbian, she replied, "I feel like a citizen of Skopje, this is the city where I was born, but I belong to the world."

Thoughts Of The Contest Winners

Busra Sarac 2nd Kahoot competition 2nd place

Hello, my name is Busra, I am doing my PhD in England on ISID and Yazidi women. I placed second in the second Kahoot competition organized by AST and wanted to briefly share my thoughts with you. It was a great pleasure for me to participate in the competition organized by AST, not only because I was second of course 😊 The questions asked were very up-to-date; it covered various topics from violence against women, to children's rights, to the fight against unlawfulness all over the world. In addition, the "Did you know these" section interspersed between the questions not only informs you about the unlawfulnesses perpetrated in and beyond Turkey, but also creates awareness. Of course, the entertaining presentation of the presenter Ms. Kubra can not be overlooked :) Thanks again and have fun everyone 😊 ■

21

Who is the educator that the MIT smuggled from Kyrgyzstan illegally and violating the rules of international law?
a) Esma Uludag
b) Orhan Inandi
c) Gökhan Açıkkollu

22

In which country is the 'Turkish Court', where victims of torture is heard by which government?
a) Sweden
b) Switzerland
c) Denmark
d) Germany

23

What is the name of the resistance that people from all walks of life started to prevent the construction of shopping malls in Turkey in 2013?
a) Gezi Park resistance
b) Izmir resistance
c) Ankara resistance

24

Who is the brave-hearted journalist imprisoned for his article "Paper Flute"?
a) Ahmet Nesin
b) Cengiz Candar
c) Hasan Cemal
d) Ahmet Altan

25 Stage 4 cancer patient, for whom AST organized the Short Film Festival, a director who passed away after being released from prison
a) Hidayet Karaca
b) Ali Unal
c) Fatih Terzioglu

27 Who is the American activist who was imprisoned and fined for voting as a woman in the presidential elections?
a) Susan B. Anthony
b) Margaret Sanger
c) Betty Ford
d) Gloria Steinman

29 There are about one billion ___ in the world. These people face barriers to accessing education, health and other services.
a) Refugee
b) Disabled
c) slave
d) Orphan and orphan

26 On what issue was Hrant Dink an active human rights defender?
a) Cooking
b) Journalism
c) Architecture
d) Law

28 Movie starring Nicholas Cage, recommended by Amnesty International for exposing arms trafficking
a) Selma
b) Black Diamond
c) God of War
d) To Kill a Mockingbird

30 When was the Human Rights Council established?
a) 2006
b) 2007
c) 1997
d) 1998

Did You Know That?

Ayşe Özdoğan

Did you know that Ayşe Özdoğan, a stage 4 cas6d7ftncer patient who has undergone many surgeries, was arrested in violation of the legal system just because she was a school administrator at Hizmet schools?

Ayşe Özdoğan and her husband were detained in Antalya on April 8, 2019 because she was an administrator at a school belonging to the Hizmet movement in Isparta. Özdoğan was released on condition of judicial control, considering the condition of her 7-year-old son, who was born with a hole in his heart.

While her husband, İlker

Özdoğan, was arrested and sent to Antalya Döşemealtı prison, Ayşe Özdoğan, whose life was turned upside down after her husband's arrest, learned that she had cancer. While taking care of her son's health and making efforts for her husband in prison, she was diagnosed with Maxillary Sinus cancer on November 7, 2019. She had surgery on her upper jaw and can only speak with a prosthesis attached to her palate. Despite her fatal and severe illness, she was brought to court shortly after her surgery and was arrested at her first hearing. Özdoğan said, "I couldn't make my voice heard to anyone."

Jeremy Seal

Did you know the British journalist and author, famous for his book about the 1960 coup and the execution of Adnan Menderes?

The name of Jeremy Seal's book is "A Coup in Turkey: A Story of Democracy, Despotism and Revenge in Divided Lands". In an interview, he explained that he believes that the Turkish people will change the government in 2023, just as they had the similar faith in the 2019 elections, and that the Turkish people are not hopeless.

Thoughts Of The Contest Winners

Ece Ozsoy 3rd Kahoot competition 3rd place

Hello everyone, I'm Ece. I am an eighth grade student in Belgium. Like you, I participated in the human rights competition held by AST last month and came in third. When we look at what is happening in our world, human rights is an important and sensitive subject that requires attention from all. I think AST gives us a great awareness by holding a competition about it. I hope you can learn something new and have fun in this competition. Good luck everyone and thanks to AST for this competition.

What is the name of the first book published by AST and offered for sale on Amazon?

3
1

a) Art for Human Rights
b) Escape from Turkey
c) Silent Scream
d) Baby in the Bag

Taraf Newspaper employee who was arrested by AKP judiciary on March 2, 2015, sentenced to 17 years and 1 month and still in prison.

3
2

a) Tuncer Cetinkaya
b) Ahmet Altan
c) Mehmet Baransu
d) Nazli Ilicak

33 Who is the girl who survived an assassination attempt by the Pakistani Taliban for fighting for the education of women?
a) Benazir Bhutto
b) Mahira Khan
c) Malala Yousafzai
d) Mehwish Life

34 In which city were the trials where the Nazis' were tried after the Second World War?
a) Munich
b) Berlin
c) Cologne
d) Nuremberg

35 What is the name of the documentary that was broadcast on Youtube on July 18, 2021 and revealed the facts of July 15?
a) Albatross
b) Orkoz
c) The Facts Are Out
d) July 15 lies

36 Solidarity platform established by a group of university students in 2020 to stand up against the increasing injustices in Turkey.
a) Other Movement
b) Enough of cruelty!
c) Freedom time
d) Resistance platform

37 Who is the news presenter, an exiled journalist and youtuber, who produces and directs the 30 Minutes program?
a) Hilal Nesin
b) Adem Yavuz Arslan
c) Erkam Tufan Aytav

38 Approximately how many languages has the Universal Declaration of Human Rights been translated into?
a) 200
b) 300
c) 400
d) 500

39 Who is the journalist and writer who was released in 2019 after being arrested after July 15 and was arrested again 8 days later?
a) Ahmet Altan
b) Mehmet Altan
c) Ali Unal
d) Engin Altan Düzyatan

40 Who is the Turkish writer, poet and journalist who was arrested for a poem criticizing Atatürk and killed by MIT?
a) Necip Fazil
b) Sabahattin Ali
c) Nazim Hikmet
d) Mehmet Akif

Did You Know That?

Mehmet Baransu

Did you know that Mehmet Baransu was arrested on charges of forming a terrorist organization without even taking his statement and was sentenced to 17 years in prison?

Mehmet Baransu's house was raided on March 2, 2015. He was arrested for providing confidential documents regarding the security of the state. So, the subject of the accusation is to obtain the sledgehammer documents, which were later cleared by the AKP judiciary for alleged fraud. Prosecutor Gökhan Gökçü referred Baransu to the court, demanding that he be arrested on the charge of establishing a terrorist organization, without even taking his statement. Baransu said to the judge who arrested him: "If I say that these documents are fake, why are you arresting me for providing confidential documents?" "If the documents are real, why are you ignoring the coup plans?" So he was sent to the 2nd High Criminal Court. They sentenced Mehmet Baransu to 17 years in prison just for doing his job. 

İbrahim & Nuran Gündüz

Did you know that two young people, who had only been married for 4 months, lost their lives in the Aegean while trying to escape from their country?

İbrahim Gündüz was a rosecutor and Nuran was a court clerk. When they both were expelled from public duty with statutory decrees. Their paths crossed years later and they got married. Exhausted by the fierce oppression, they decided to leave their country on December 2, 2021. While they were trying to cross the region, they were both capsized and two young people departed this life together at the spring of their lives.

Thoughts Of The Contest Winners

Nefise Nihal Gonul 1st Kahoot Competition 2nd Place

Hey there! I'm Nefise Nihal, and let me tell you about an awesome experience I had two years back—I won an AST Kahoot contest, and scored a prize!

It wasn't just about winning; it was a blast of quick decision-making and strategic thinking. Plus, I got to co-host with Kubra abla, which was super cool! This contest wasn't just a game; it was a mix of fun and learning. It challenged me to think fast and make sharp decisions. Being a part of the behind-the-scenes action as a co-host also showed me the effort that goes into such events. I totally recommend others to give it a shot too!

Furkan Cakin 2nd Kahoot Competition 3rd Place

Hi everyone! I'm joining from New Hampshire today. In the last AST Kahoot game, which was about three weeks ago I believe, I came in third place and earned $100. It was actually very productive and educational, and I learned a lot. I think you should definitely check it out. Their contests are not just Kahoot games, they have a lot of different contests that you can join as well. The latest one I've seen so far was the international art contest, where they were giving out a thousand dollars for first place, and I believe $500 for second and third, and so on. They also give away a lot of gifts just for participating in the contests, which is great. I've been following AST for two years now, and I believe that they are doing a great job addressing human rights, guarding civil, political, economic, social, and cultural rights as well. They organize a lot of events, publish a lot of articles that you should definitely check out, and you can follow them on social media if you want. If you want to donate to them, you should definitely do that as well. So, from me, I would suggest you totally check out their website and try to join the Kahoot game. The next one is going to be on Sunday at 12pm, I don't know exactly, but they have great gifts and great opportunities for better students who would also like to do an internship or anything like that. If you want to do any community service, they will definitely help you out with that as well. They have so many activities that you could actually utilize. That's it from me now, but thank you so much AST for doing such a good job!

41 Which of the following did not fight for the civil rights of African Americans?
a) Martin Luther King Jr.
b) Rosa Parks
c) Morgan Freeman
d) Malcom X

42 On what date is Human Rights Day celebrated each year?
a) December 10
b) October 23
c) June 7
d) November 18

44 Which country has not yet ratified the Convention on the Rights of the Child, which was signed and ratified by 192 countries in 1995?
a) Türkiye
b) United States
c) India
d) Iraq

43 According to the data of the Occupational Health and Safety Council, at least how many people died in Turkey in work accidents in the first 10 months of 2021?
a) 2560
b) 477
c) 1853
d) 790

45 What is the basic human right that the Prophet Muhammad (PBUH) mentioned in the first place in his Farewell Sermon?
a) The right to freedom
b) Right to work
c) The right to entertainment
d) Right to life

46 According to IHD and TIHV data, at least how many women were killed as a result of male violence in the first 11 months of 2021?
a) 80
b) 120
c) 260
d) 290

47

Who is the prosecutor from the Decree Law, who lost his life together with his wife as a result of the boat capsizing while trying to cross to Greece?
a) Mustafa Kara
b) Hüseyin Maden
c) İbrahim Gündüz
d) Cemil Karabidek

48

Which one is not one of the novels of Sabahattin Ali, who was killed while fleeing the political pressures he was experiencing in Turkey?
a) Yusuf from Kuyucak
b) Madonna in a Fur Coat
c) Canan
d) The Devil Within

49

Who is the Italian artist who painted the photograph of Mustafa Enis Durak hugging his mother in the court corridor on the street wall?
a) Thomas Nast
b) İbrahim Özdabak
c) Matt Groening
d) Gianluca Constantine

50

Name and place of the association founded by a group of university students during World War II to explain the mistakes of the war.
a) Reds - Berlin
b) Young Germans - Berlin
c) White Roses - Munich
d) Greens - Cologne

Did You Know That?

Uyghur Genocide

Did you know that more than 1 million Uyghur Muslims are being held in secret detention camps without any legal process?

Uyghur genocide is a name given to the violence and human rights violations committed against Uyghurs by the Chinese Communist Party. This genocide led to the detention of more than 1 million Muslims, the majority of whom were Uyghurs, in secret detention camps without legal process. Many activists, human rights experts, and government officials call this incident a genocide. The violence against Uyghurs is considered to be the highest number of people getting arrested, subjected to violence, and killed due to their ethnic and religious identities since World War Two.

Mustafa Enis Durak

Did you know that university student, Mustafa Enis Durak was arrested 3 times in 6 months?

Mustafa Enis Durak came second at Maltepe Military school in 2014. After the Military school was closed, he entered the medical school at Muğla Sıtkı Koçman University. Durak's 3rd year at the medical school had to be left unfinished because he was arrested for the third time in six months. He is currently in prison. Italian painter Gianluca Costantini, known for his drawings on human rights violations, draws Mustafa Enis Durak's last farewell to his mother on the wall of Leblebici Street in Beyoğlu. In his last arrest, Mustafa Enis Durak was sentenced to seven years and six months in prison. ▪

Thoughts Of The Contest Winners

Muberra Duman 6th Kahoot Competition 3rd place

I really like the kahoot competitions at the end of AST's broadcast programs. By following the content carefully and regardless of the speed factor, competition becomes both fun and profitable. I also came 3rd in the kahoot competition in the program about human rights. I received my award within the same week. I would like to thank AST and its volunteers very much, more importantly than my medal, for being a defender of human rights and writing in golden letters in the history of these legal services... ▪

🎙 INTERVIEW: "Journalist Adem Yavuz Arslan, we discussed the human rights violations related to his and his colleague, Journalist-Writer Mehmet Baransu's imprisonment both before and after the coup attempt in Turkey."

💬 **Kubra Unver:** I would like to welcome his colleague journalist Adem Yavuz Arslan to tell us about journalist-author Mehmet Baransu, who has been imprisoned for 7 years, to whom we have dedicated this month. As David Letterman said in his show on Netflix "My next guest need no introduction" Welcome Mr. Adem, thank you very much again for joining our program, you have added color, we know that you have worked on many different topics. When Adem Yavuz Arslan is mentioned, we think of a journalist-writer, but could you introduce yourself to us for our young friends who may be listening to you for the

first time or who want to learn more about you?

💬 **Adem Yavuz Arslan:** Hello everyone, I am young too, so please don't present me as retired and I have not retired yet, I am one of those who feel young even though we are older. Because youth is something that happens in the mind. I have been practicing journalism for more or less 30 years, I studied at the Faculty of Communication. There were faculties of communication in Turkey. I think they still exist now. I studied as a first choice, so a career in journalism was primarily a goal for me. I directly preferred the Faculty of Communication and while I was at school, I started working as a police-courthouse reporter at the courthouse. I mean, I was at the courthouse from morning to night, watching the hearings and trials, writing news from there, I interviewed people at every stage of life, while I was working as a police reporter, now young friends may not remember that reality shows are very famous in Turkey. In the American media, there are still night police reporters, murders, conflicts, bloodshed, I did a lot of that work and I even used to joke that if I saw less than five dead bodies a day, it was not a good day for me, so I said I didn't see enough dead bodies today, I did news like that for years, I watched the invasion of Iraq, I watched the Kosovo conflicts, the work I did with the refugees there was published by the United Nations as a photo exhibition in Turkey and in Athens, and it was published in Greece and it was published in Greece, and there are awards I received from there, there is not a job I have not done as a journalist, I mean, I have worked as a political reporter in Ankara for many years, including sports photojournalism. TV programs with politicians, travels, I mean, I have

TV programs with Erdoğan and all AKP executives and other opposition party leaders, I have photographs with all of them, and later they were used in a different way, that's why I'm telling you the photographs as a joke, and in 2014 I had to move to the United States because of the cases I was following and the books I published and wrote, I have published three books so far and I am in trouble because of these books. You have to look for a journalist who is not in trouble in Turkey, you are either in prison or in exile. I had to move to America in 2014 because it was obvious that Mehmet Baransu's story, which I will tell in a moment, was about to happen to me. We moved to America in 2014 to Washington, I have been here since that day, my passport was canceled after I came from Turkey, there are lawsuits against me with life imprisonment and life imprisonment, there are some accusations such as being wanted with an international red notice, why are there, because the books we write, the publications we write, the principles we defend, especially the corrupt leaders are very disturbing, especially all the areas I work in, that is, both the Deep State in Turkey, that is, the people who do dirty work, disturbed and disturbed the government very much, I have been here

for seven years in America. I continue to work as a journalist in the US, so even though our newspapers have been shut down, it is easy for those who have something to say to find a way to walk on social media, you know, if you just want to walk, you can find a way, you can work, social media, new technologies, apps provide unlimited opportunities, so if they put a barrier in front of you, you can hang that barrier twice more. I was giving photography lessons to high school friends around Washington, which has always been a wound in my heart, and we did a 10-week workshop for friends here. I have a considerable background in photography, I have given photography lessons before, and I have photography awards and photography exhibitions. My expectation is that the human rights violations in Turkey will end a little bit, Turkey will normalize a little bit and I will focus more on taking photographs because taking photographs is also a passion for me and I have a special interest in photography, I strongly recommend it to the audience friends, photography is a magnificent art, a magnificent field, and I insist on those who are curious about photography, take an interest in photography, it will open a completely different door for you.

Kubra Unver: Thank you very much, we exchange ideas with friends on what can be done for human rights in every program. Thank you for giving us new ideas and at the same time for updating your profile that we know. Now we would like to get to know Mehmet Baransu a little bit. Would you like to give us some information about who he is?

Adem Yavuz Arslan: Mehmet Baransu is a journalist, we worked together for about two years 1999-200. I shared the same desk with Mehmet Baransu, that is, our computers were side by side and we worked together at Aksiyon magazine. He was from Erzurum or Kars, if I remember correctly, he was of Kurdish origin, he was studying at Istanbul Communication or Marmara Communication. He was a person who liked to take care of things, and when he worked together, the files he made, the subjects he worked on were always such subjects. He signed very important news, he received awards, he has really prestigious awards in Turkey, especially prestigious awards such as the Sedat Simavi journalism award, a friend who has gone down in the history of Turkey with his news. Unfortunately, he has been in prison for seven years and there is a government that especially enjoys mistreating him.

Kubra Unver: Yes I understand, thank you very much Mehmet Baransu, we know he is a journalist, so why is he a successful journalist?

Adem Yavuz Arslan: Why is it successful, first of all, it's very important to be brave in journalism because the news you report, I mean, let me put it this way, there's a phrase that's said in communication faculties or journalism schools, there's a lot of clichés that are written in the books, "news is what the politicians, the powerful people, don't want to be spread." So you're uncovering something that they're hiding and you're publishing it on behalf of the public, that's why journalists are not liked anyway, because newspapers are a threat everywhere, it's like this everywhere in the world. It is the same in America, it is the same in other countries. Now why are you, Baransu, a good journalist?

First of all because you are brave, because the news you find and the subjects you work on are dangerous subjects. Turkey is a country where journalists are murdered, last week was the anniversary of the murder of Hrant Dink. A country where journalists are arrested, we are even ahead of China in this regard, we are one ahead of Russia, we are the world champion by far, so there is no one close to us, there is no one who can come close to us in this regard. Now if you are a journalist you have a choice, you can either propagandize for the government, which is not journalism, like the people who are doing journalism in Turkey now, or you can do real journalism, like Baransu and other friends of mine, but this time you will not get out of trouble, you can be imprisoned, your family will be victimized, your wife and children will be victimized, because we have seen examples of this, unfortunately there were journalist friends whose spouses were arrested along with them, or you have to go into exile, or you have to live abroad, like me. Everything you have in Turkey has been confiscated, they confiscate all your savings, they victimized your family, but the most basic point is that if you ask what Baransu brings to the forefront when describing him, I would say courage. He is really a very brave friend because many of our young friends did not live through these periods, we did not live through the coup of September 12, followed by the postmodern coup of February 28, especially in those years, the early 2000 years, there was a really terrible atmosphere of fear in Turkey. Now it is a different issue, but it is appropriate that it was something else and it was really great courage to be able to write the news that Baransu wrote about the issues he wrote about in those days, because when you write, you cannot foresee what will happen to you, you can be arrested, you can be killed, a bomb can be sent to your address, for example, it was sent to my address, to my house, I mean, because of the books I wrote. One day a package arrived, pretending to be a book. When I opened it, Kalashnikov bullets came out of it and there was a death threat. Not every journalist may want to deal with such things, some journalists hesitate. He is afraid, he doesn't have the courage, but it is this courage that distinguishes Baransu from the others and makes him special in a way, because he has reported about them in all areas where the military is very powerful, the mafia leaders who do the dirty work are very powerful, the corrupt politicians are very powerful, and corrupt politicians are very powerful, so he is very important.

💬 Kubra Unver: Even when you hear what you are talking about, people get goosebumps, at least I was very impressed when I was listening to it, the fact that you continue your work and try to publish accurate news despite the threats you receive, I want to say that I am glad that you and other journalists like Mehmet Baransu exist, unfortunately we know that he has been imprisoned for years, what is the reason why Mehmet Baransu, who has been imprisoned for nearly 37 years for his verified news reports, has still not been released?

💬 Adem Yavuz Arslan: Let me first remind you about the news stories for which Mehmet Baransu was sentenced and the news stories for

which he is on trial. What would we live without Mehmet Baransu is really a very important question, what would we do without Baransu. For example, one of Mehmet Baransu's news reports is that there is a Kurdish problem in Turkey, there is a terrorism problem, there is a deep state problem, in other words, there is a deep state, some young friends, especially those who grew up in the west, may not understand the deep state, the structure we call the deep state is water; mafia organizations or dirty people who have settled inside the state, they commit murders, they plant bombs, they target innocent people, these are the main motivations behind human rights violations, let me give you an example, for example, Christian minorities in Turkey in 2005, they were very targeted and this targeting was followed by murders, the murder of Hrant Dink, the murder of Zirve in Malatya, other examples came, this was an operation of the deep state in Turkey. The deep state says that person X is a target, is an enemy, must be destroyed and while doing this, public opinion is created, social media sites are set up. Virtual fake websites are opened and for example, there was a priest in Turkey, he was a priest of a church and this priest was appearing on the screens every day and he was making statements saying that Turkish youth were being turned into Christians, I went to this person, he was a priest in Mersin, I interviewed him and talked to him. I finally published the document that this man is actually a military intelligence officer, a man of the deep state commissioned by the state to make provocations in these affairs, of course there was a lot of controversy. So imagine that you are a church pastor but the man is actually a soldier (Soldier) and his job is this pastoral provocation Now Baransu's news is always like this, for example, one of them was the coup plan, that is, the cage plan, the Sledgehammer Action Plan, or the Sledgehammer Operation Plan, or the coup plans in Turkey, it is very important because it deciphered the coup plans, so a wissir blovirlar is very common in America, it is common in other countries. wissir blovirlik and journalism, it broke a very important ground in my opinion. People in Turkey would think that four soldiers were martyred if it wasn't for Baransu, because the state said that four soldiers were martyred and killed by PKK militants, but in reality these soldiers were not martyred, but one psychopathic maniac commanding a soldier El If you pull the pin of that grenade, it will explode after a certain period of time and no one can hold it in their hands for a long time. Four soldiers lost their lives because of the action of this psychopathic commander. Baransu published his information and documented it and was given an award for it. If it wasn't for Baransu, we would be asking about the deaths of these soldiers in Turkey as a result of clashes between the PKK and terrorist organizations. For example, there is one of them, for example, the Dağlıca Aktütün police station in the Southeast of Turkey, which was raided by PKK members and dozens of soldiers were killed there, but did it really happen? In 2006, the country's Chief of General Staff That's why the Taraf newspaper broke new ground, don't look back from today, people talk more freely today because of the effect of social media, they write more freely today. There was no social media in those years, and to do this kind of news, I mean, you have to be very serious, you have to be very brave, because you can be destroyed by an accident in the morning, by a bomb in a month, you can be arrested by an act that looks like an accident, which is already seven years in prison and there is no such thing, why is Baransu not being released? There are two main reasons behind Baransu not being released, but there are two enemies at once, either there is no government regime for me, that is, the change of Erdogan, and secondly, the deep state in Turkey, because Baransu has been fighting with both of them together, and today both sides continue to keep him in prison with the concert sauce in common. That's why he was arrested, it has nothing to do with it, they are lying. Baransu is under arrest for publishing a secret document of the state. Baransu is arrested for publishing a secret document of the state and what you call a secret document is this. For example, how is the power of renaissance or there are other examples, so you are doing wissir blovurluk, when we publish a secret document of the state, this is something that is a journalist, for example, in America you cannot make such a trial, you cannot accuse journalists like this, but you cannot do it in Europe, it has not been done in Turkey yet.The main motivation behind Baransu not being released for all these years is that these two enemies, the deep state and the dirty murderous state in Turkey, as well as the Erdogan regime, have reached a common agreement and Baransu is still in prison and do you know the reason for his arrest? It is a very grave picture, Baransu is in prison because of a news that was not published, there is a news that was not published, there is a claim that a

call Baransu, I still laugh when I remember it, so we didn't use the name Baransu instead Okaca, because he looked like a Nigerian footballer. He was also a little dark and he played football well. I hope he will be saved as soon as possible and he will return to the field again. I remember we played many football matches

coup plan was published and there is a claim that that plan was destroyed, but for 6 years he has not been able to prove that that coup plan was published .Prosecutor because no such news was published, he is in prison because of the news that was not published.

Kubra Unver: Thank you very much, can you share a memory you had with him?

Adem Yavuz Arslan: We never used the name Mehmet for Baransu, I don't know why, we've been going by Baransu since day one, we've been going by his surname Baransu's nickname for us was Okaca. Okaca was a Nigerian footballer who played for Fenerbahçe and he was very similar to Baransu In our newspaper and magazine, everyone used to

with him although I had a jubilee because I broke my foot in a match, but I know he continued for years. He was really interested in football.

Kubra Unver: We wish him a speedy acquittal like all our other friends who are in prison and Adem Bey thank you very much for taking the time to contribute to our awareness. We wish you a good day.

Adem Yavuz Arslan: Thank you, I would like to ask you to continue such activities because it is very important to raise awareness, I mean, the struggle for Human Rights is a whole, it can only be done by raising awareness, so I think it is useful to continue such activities. Thank you, see you soon.

51 The name of the golden yellow cobblestones laid in European countries to remember the victims of World War II.
a) Reminder stones
b) Landmarks
c) Memory stones
d) Stumbling stones

52 Who is the author of the book "A Coup in Turkey"?
a) Jeremy Seal
b) John Dahl
c) Ali Bulac
d) Nevval Sevindi

53 Who is the author of the book "Silent Scream" published by AST?
a) AST
b) Mina Leyla
c) Dogan Yucel
d) Hafza Girdap

54 A film about the friendship between a German commander's child and a Jewish child in a concentration camp during World War II?
a) Schindler's List
b) Piano Piano Child
c) Life is Beautiful
d) The Boy in the Striped Pajamas

55 Which of the following is recognized as a basic human right by the Universal Declaration of Human Rights, ensuring the right of individuals to participate in the government of their country?
a) Right to arbitrary arrest
b) Right to freedom of speech
c) Right to vote in free and fair elections
d) Right to forced labor

56 Aziz Nesin's novel, inspired by a true story, about politicians deceiving the public, and adapted for cinema.
a) Karabela
b) Zübuk
c) Seat
d) Hamdi the Elephant

5 7

Where is Nadia Murad, who was awarded the Nobel peace prize in 2018, from?
a) Iran
b) Iraq
c) Afghanistan
d) Pakistan

5 8

The association was founded by the Prophet Muhammad (PBUH) with the youth of Mecca with the aim of protecting the weak and powerless and preventing oppression.
a) Uzzab-ul Mecca
b) Medinetu-l Fazila
c) Al-adlu-l Mecca
d) Hilf-ul Fudul

5 9

What is the name of the biographical work written by Mina Leyla from AST, about the life of teacher Gökhan Açıkkollu?
a) A Martyrdom Composition
b) The Painful Story of a Teacher
c) They killed you too
d) My Gokhan, You Didn't Die

6 0

The woman who died in Iran after the violence she was subjected to by the morality police for not obeying the dress code.
a) Mahira Khan
b) Malala Yousafzai
c) Mahsa Amini
d) Mehwish Life

Did You Know That?

George Floyd

Did you know that a Black citizen lost his life due to a police officer strangling him for 6 minutes?

The police came upon a report that Floyd had given a fake $20 bill. In return, the police pressed his knee on George Floyd's neck while Floyd was handcuffed on the ground. No matter how many times Floyd repeated that he could not breathe, the police did not take him seriously causing Floyd to die in 6 minutes. This event became a great spark for the Black Lives Matter movement in the United States. Although slavery was abolished in 1865 and institutional discrimination was made a federal crime due to the civil rights struggle in the 1960s, racism continues in America, especially for Black citizens. 

Osman Kavala

Did you know that Osman Kavala is still unlawfully imprisoned for a case, in which he was found not guilty twice?

Osman Kavala is the only detained defendant in the Gezi Çarşı case. Kavala, who was detained on October 18, 2017 has been detained since November 1, 2017 on charges of financing the Gezi events. Kavala applied to the Constitutional Court in the second month of his detention, and to the European Court of Human Rights in his eighth month. However, Kavala, was detained again by the Istanbul Chief Public Prosecutor's Office from the same case he had previously been released from. On March 9, Istanbul Criminal Court arrested Osman Kavala within the scope of the same investigation, but this time on charges of espionage. The provisions of the European Court of Human Rights stating that Osman Kavala's detention should end were not fulfilled. On the fourth anniversary of his arrest, the ambassadors of 10 countries, including the United States, jointly signed the call for Kavala's release. Reacting harshly to the call, President Erdoğan made serious accusations against Kavala. As a result, he remains in detention despite the decision of the European Court of Human Rights. ■

İsa Altekin 5th Kahoot competition 1st. Place

Greetings to everyone from Argentina!
First of all, thank you very much for what you have done and the work you have accumulated. When I learned journalist Adem Yavuz Arslan was a guest speaker, I decided to join the 5th Kahoot Human Rights competition. His hospitality attracted my attention.

I would also like to thank AST for the first prize in the competition, which I participated in under the pseudonym "Jesus" (it took some effort to enter the competition).

I am a follower of AST and pray for the end of cruelty on mankind." ■

🎤 INTERVIEW: Journalist Arbana Xharra shared with us the human rights violations experienced before and after the torture and subsequent murder of Kurdish politician Garibe Gezer, who was convicted of terrorism and sentenced to life imprisonment. She also provided advice for human rights activists."

💬 **Kubra Unver:** Hi Arbana, welcome to our program and thank you for joining us today to introduce Garibe Gezer to us. I have briefly introduced Garibe Gezer, a Kurdish female politician, although when I google her the first thing that pops-up is her being a prisoner or political inmate, but I know she had a bigger story than that. Including our audience, we would like to know her closely. Can you introduce us to Garibe Gezer and tell us who she was?

💬 **Arbana Xharra:** Hi and thank you for inviting me and i'm honored to talk here today and as you've mentioned it's so unfortunate because if you google you do not see her name on the major media international media or major international human rights organization so you have some of the local news a local ngos that they've been raising the question of what happened to gaza.

So she was a young kurdish activist and she's been raising her voice against the regime dictatorship on requesting the rights of the kurdish people that they are suffering for decades now. She was convicted of terrorism charges in 2016 and sentenced to life in prison without pearl within an additional 2 years and she's been telling her family and her lawyers that she's been abused within the jail by the guard so she faced sexual harassment and a lot of abuse.

No one really cared about what happened to her even though the people's democratic party representative and the human rights association of Turkey brought a motion to investigate her treatment in prison before the parliament on october 25 of the last year. But no one really was interested to investigate her case because her case tells the whole story on what is happening with the kurdish activists within the prison. She is not the only one that died in the prison; there are many other Kurdish female and male activists and politicians that are finding their death and no one is really investigating what is happening. Despite this, no one investigated so she remained in the prison until her death. It's very sad to read and find out what happened to her, and the lack of the interest to investigate further. So this is the clear message to the other human rights activists, politicians, those who have courage to raise their voice on what is going on with kurds, not to do so because they are going to face death and at the end of the day they are saying that she killed herself. No one knows exactly what happened, there are other prisoners that send the letter saying that she was killed but no one is really interested to find out because this is a system, that is what they are doing to the kurdish people. Garibe Gezer also criticized Turkish decision to leave the Istanbul convention on the Council of Europe treaty that aims to fight violence against women. She raised her voice, even though she was a local politician, she raised her voice on the major things related to all the women, not only kurdish, but all the women in turkey. It was so powerful to hear that raising a voice for a cause can actually, you know, save someone's life and because a number of people fail to do so unfortunately we don't have Garibe Gezer

among us. She already told about how she experienced torture and sexual violence to her lawyer, so this is sad because we had her voice telling what is going on within the prison, what's happened to her. If it is what happened to her, it's happening to other prisoners. She was 21 when she died last year and she had so much courage to raise her voice and to come against the whole system, against the guards in the prison and against the whole system that made her suffer and made many, many other kurdish females and other male prisoners to face what she was facing. It is so sad. What should we do? It's to use all the opportunities to raise the voice, to ask for the major media outlets to report on this because we need to grab the attention of the E.U leaders because we know that the Turkish system, the government, the president, this is what they are doing. They want to hide the reality, so we need the N.G.Os, the human rights organization, journalists, but we need to ask and find the network within the major media outlets and bring this to shed light on what is going on. This is the case, this is one case, Garibe Gezer, we know what happened to her. It is so sad when i have find out that also they refused to transport her body after she was killed, saying that she committed the suicide. How can we seek justice when the society, when the people there were not supporting her cause except her family raising their voice and her lawyer that they couldn't do anything more. If everyone else is silent, what about others right now that are in prison? They are going to have the same faith and no one really cares.

The audience, whoever is listening to us, just go and google this name and see who reported about this case, see if the international audience knows. No, they don't know and this is very sad. Where are the human rights organizations, women rights organizations to raise their voice. Just because she was the local activist, now everyone is remaining silent?

This is very sad, and I'm going to use this opportunity to ask for all my connections, my colleagues, the human rights organization, to see, investigate, and ask for the response, what happened to Garibe Gezer. What is happening to the other Kurdish women that are being killed within the prison just because they are raising their voice for their basic rights? Why does the world remain silent on what the Kurdish people are facing for decades now? The systematic prosecution of the Kurdish community denying their basic human rights. What if this happened in the western countries, what if an activist and a politician, the human rights activist, got killed in suspicious circumstances. Would they report? Yes! Why not when it comes to the Kurdish people? We need to find a way to ask for the biden administration to raise its voice and focus on what is happening and what is still all what they are facing, all the prosecution that The Kurdish people are facing with no international support. Yeah, especially given the fact that Kurdish people are the largest stateless ethnicity, it is our responsibility as citizens of the world to raise our voice. It doesn't have to be just reaching out to the biggest media outlet and reporting, but even like opening the conversation and starting from brainstorming the questions you just asked. Like you asked so many beautiful questions for us to open the conversation and graduate students can write their thesis and bachelor students can ask these questions to their professors and get their opinion. There are so many things that can be done.

The thing is that I mentioned major media outlets because the regime shut down over 130 television channels, radio stations, newspapers, and magazines. They have arrested over 231 journalists who are going to report there, that's why I mentioned.

The purge has inflicted suffering on more than like millions of people, so their family is the door that they can go and seek for justice if Gazelle had the courage to raise her voice and see what happened to her. As I said, she was convicted on terrorism charges and sentenced to life sentence without parole, with an additional 21 years.

This is the clear message sent to other potential human rights activists see what is going to happen to you in case you raise your voice about your rights, so that's why we should stand beside them. They need our moral support, they need our support and we have to use our potential, all our networks and help them. I am an analyst, someone else coming from a different field so we need to raise our voices.

💬 Kubra Unver: Thank you, you briefly mentioned why she was an important activist and politician in turkey. So if you could like elaborate on that a little bit more and tell us some of the contributions she did to the region of the arbor or Turkey overall and she must have done something to get on someone's nerves to end up in jail so can you tell us also what happened to Garibe Gezer.

💬 Arbana Xharra: So, she started her activism in her town where she used to live, and then in the beginning she was very active within her small circle, and then she started raising her voice against the Erdogan regime on what he was doing to all the kurdish but also to the turkish people after in 2016 and the cult that

happened and the harassment. So she started raising her voice on the national level. As soon as she started raising her voice on the national level attacking directly the Erdogan regime, then they had seen her potential that she might have a lot of influence in the society because she went beyond her local problems. Like raising her voice on poverty and what the Kurdish people are facing in women rights and then as I said she's been criticizing the decision of Erdogan that affected women. That affected Kurdish women, that affected Turkish women, and so she went beyond the local problems. So that's why they have seen that her voice is getting higher and higher and that's why they wanted her silence. Then as they usually do, they convict you based on the terrorism charges. So this is what exactly happened to her, as soon as she had courage to directly attack Erdogan on what he is doing to the Kurds and what he's doing to the people that raised their voice based on human rights. I think that at that point they immediately convicted her to silence her and through her to silence other human rights activists. Yeah, so this also tells us why she was an important figure in human rights and she actually made a change, and because she could make a change this kind came along with her fate.

💬 Kubra Unver: Lastly, I would like to leave this conversation with an action plan. You have already made some recommendations to the international level of the figures and systems what they can do to prevent similar instant incidents to cure. What would you recommend to the Turkish government and also as young human activists we also would like to

contribute something, like any social cause that might be interesting to us. So what would be your recommendations?

💬 **Arbana Xharra:** I know how hard it is within Turkey to raise the voice and criticize the government. I know what they're going to be faced with as soon as they raise their voice, so as I mentioned the people's democratic party and other human rights associations within Turkey they can use their institutional ways to ask for investigation, but it is more important as you mentioned to open the debate. There are different ways to open the debate, not just in turkey but also outside within the universities, the Turkish community, the Kurdish community, the youth, they all share the same problems. Kurds and Turks that are facing problems right now with the Erdogan's regime, they need to come closer with each other because they both have the same problem. We cannot ignore Kurds just because we are not Kurds, I'm talking right now about the Turkish people, the turkish association, the turkish human rights activists, there are brilliant writers, there are brilliant professors in the united states among the E.U. We have to ask them to write, we need to bring the light in these cases by raising our voice. The user can organize debates, there are social media, they cannot prevent you by speaking as we are doing right now via zoom. We need to inform people first of all on what is going on in order to raise awareness. We need to have consistency in raising awareness, we cannot just organize this debate and then forget about what happened. We need to speak loud through the social media within the universities, if in Turkey it's not possible because i know if you organize a protest the organizer will be arrested and sent to jail. I know how hard it is, and I applaud all of them that have the courage within that awful and ruthless dictatorship that they are living to raise their voice, but there are also other ways that we can be activated and raise awareness. Given the fact that our audience is pretty international here, those who can practice their fundamental freedom of speech in their current places could be actually very practical steps too. I would like to just mention my personal case. I've been writing a lot on what the Erdogan regime was doing outside Turkey, especially in Kosovo, where I come from they've been trying to silence me in different ways.I've been physically attacked, they find out where I live and they come and they draw the red cross next to my apartment. My son was seven when he saw the red cross drawn next to the door where we used to live. Now what they are doing is the media that are sponsored by the Erdogan regime every day. They do fake news against me just to silence me and they use different ways to silence critical voices and I know that it's not just me there are many many more out there that are trying to raise awareness and we cannot stop. I would like to thank you on behalf of our audience and also myself that I'm standing firm and standing tall and showing us that despite the consequences we should not give up. We can still keep going and make a change.

💬 **Kubra Unver: Thank you again Arbana for making the time for us and exploring this specific case more in depth and leaving us with an action plan of what we can do.** ▪

61 Saturday Mothers is a community that organizes sit-ins and searches for the perpetrators of their relatives who disappeared in custody.
a) True
b) False

62 Identify the fundamental human right established by the Universal Declaration of Human Rights that ensures individuals are protected from torture and cruel, inhuman, or degrading treatment or punishment.
a) Right to slavery
b) Right to education
c) Right to freedom of assembly
d) Right to freedom from torture

63 Which of the following rights, outlined in the Universal Declaration of Human Rights, emphasizes the right of everyone to own property alone as well as in association with others?
a) Right to child labor
b) Right to freedom of religion
c) Right to private property
d) Right to forced displacement

64 What is the name of the Kurdish woman whose death under police custody sparked nationwide demonstrations in Iran, resulting in global attention?
a) Nazanin Boniadi
b) Masih Alinejad
c) Mahsa Amini
d) Narges Mohammadi

65 Who is the American human rights activist who wrote a doctoral thesis on the social genocide in Turkey in December 2023 and was accepted with high honor?
a) Kemm Sarver
b) Karl O'Rourke
c) Nancy Larins
d) Emma Watson

66 What is the best answer about Torture?
a) Is allowed if used to prevent terrorist attacks
b) Is only allowed after the decision of a judge
c) It is never allowed

67 A person who leaves their country because of persecutions due to race, religion, nationality, political or social group are referred as?
a) Immigrant
b) Refugee
c) Disadvantaged person
d) Alien

68 Who sets out international human rights standards?
a) International Red Cross
b) Governments of individual countries
c) United Nations
d) Amnesty International

69 Turkey's withdrawal from the Council of Europe Convention on Preventing and Combating Violence against Women and Domestic Violence (Istanbul Convention) in 2021 has emboldened perpetrators, and left victims at increased risk regarding?
a) Intimate partner violence
b) Femicide
c) Child marriages
d) All of the above

70 Who was co-leader of the Peoples' Democratic Party (HDP), and imprisoned since November 2016?
a) Selahattin Demirtas
b) Yasar Kemal
c) Sezgin Tanrikulu

Did You Know That?

Garibe Gezer

Did you know about the inhumane treatment that Garibe Gezer experienced, both in prison and after her death?

Garibe Gezer was 23 years old when she was the director of the Democratic Regions Party in the Dargeçit district of Mardin and was arrested 5 years ago. While she was transferred to Kandıra Prison, she was subjected to serious torture, rape, and harassment. Garibe Gezer wanted to convey this to her family and lawyers, but she was put in a cell for 22 days. After leaving the cell, she wanted to write a letter, but since she did not obey, she was taken to a sponge room and her last resort was to tell it to her family through the phone. Following the criminal complaint, 22 female deputies from HDP submitted a parliamentary question to the Ministry of Justice, asking for the allegations to be investigated and informed that Garibe Gezer committed suicide and lost her life in a solitary cell. Gezer's body is sent to Mardin by a cargo plane, where the family is not given a hearse causing Gezer to be transported by a truck.

Mahsa Amini

Did you know that Mahsa Amini was killed because she wasn't complying with the headscarf rules in Iran?

Mahsa Amini is taken to the hospital in a coma after being detained by the Irshad patrols, known as the morality police in Iran, on September 13th. She passed away on September 16th. The reason she was attacked by the morality police was because she wasn't complying with the headscarf rules in Iran. Everyone has the freedom of thought, religion and conscience as stated in the 2nd and 18th articles of the Universal Declaration of Human Rights, this includes choosing to wear or not to wear a religious headscarf. Any interventions in these rights would be absolute injustice.

Thoughts Of The Contest Winners

Muhammet Kemal 5th Kahoot competition 2nd place

Hello everyone,

I won second place in the 5th Kahoot contest on human rights organized by the AST. Since my first participation in the second contest, I never missed the opportunity to participate in this engaging contest. I trust that this contest is a great learning and revision opportunity about human rights issues especially in Turkey. I hope God gives the strength and wisdom to defend these universal rights to all human rights defenders around the world. I want to thank all the valuable members of the AST team for organizing such a motivational contest and of course for the award. Thank you!

Emine Kose Yuce 7th Kahoot competition 2nd place

It is a great contribution of these Kahoot competitions to bring awareness on historic deterioration. While the fact that it is award-winning increases the incentive especially among students, the publications during the competition also provide an opportunity to find out whether we are aware of many similar events that we do not know about. For these enthusiasts, it helps them look more carefully at past and current versions and consider them from a broader perspective. We cannot see the efforts of the team working as friends to continue the competitions for a few intervals. Just as they are an important source of resources for all of us on how spiritual support can be, we need to remember their contribution to a more positive flow of history. It's like one of the bees that flap their wings to keep the atmosphere of the hive suitable for the colony. A small but effective contribution. Thank you and greetings to everyone who struggles to be together with good and stay away from evil.

🎙 INTERVIEW: Judge Kemal Karanfil, we discussed the great sensitivity with which he performed his duties before the July 15th incident, as well as the injustices and human rights violations he experienced afterwards. Additionally, we obtained advice for young people regarding human rights violations.

💬 **Kubra Unver:** Welcome, Mr. Kemal.

💬 **Kemal Karanfil:** Thank you, hello.

💬 **Kubra Unver:** How are you?

💬 **Kemal Karanfil:** Thank you very much, to be here makes me feel better. How are you?

💬 **Kubra Unver: Doing very well. Whenever we host a program, I get very excited. Talking to our participants and seeing guest speakers among us, adds color and enjoyment to the program. Thank you for coming.**

💬 **Kemal Karanfil:** I thank you.

💬 **Kubra Unver: Now, you are active on social media, especially on Twitter and YouTube, and your profile reflects a significant background in the field of law. You share effective content related to human rights and injustices. Can you introduce yourself to our listeners, especially to our young friends?**

💬 **Kemal Karanfil:** Certainly, with pleasure. I was born on January 6, 1972, in Siirt. I am the fourth child of an officer working for the municipality, among 11 siblings. Due to limited financial means, I attended middle school at a Boarding Primary School in Şirvan after which I took the free boarding exams and got accepted to Ankara Hotel and Tourism Vocational High School. I completed my studies there and graduated at the top of my class. However, I

initially went to Tourism High School with the idea of becoming an interpreter or something similar. But when I learned that the school trained individuals for professional service in five-star hotels, I didn't choose that path. I entered the university entrance exam (ÖSYM) for law faculty and was accepted. In 1998, I took the judge exam. Initially, I wanted to become an assistant professor at the university, but unfortunately, in Turkey, candidates from specific families are often preferred, so I was consistently eliminated in interviews. It seems destiny was for me to become a judge. In 1998, I also took the first judge exam organized by ÖSYM and performed well. Back then, they were supposed to hire 500 judges, but only 425 were selected out of 10,000 candidates, which was quite challenging. After a two-and-a-half-year internship, I started working in Burdur, then in Olur district of Erzurum, and later in Germencik district of Aydın. I chose the Court of Appeals after being encouraged by the President of the Honorary 13th Chamber of the Court of Appeals, Mr. Seyret Atalay, who is also from my hometown. But I regretted that decision. However, leaving the Court of Appeals is not easy; if the President likes you, you are kept there. I managed to leave after five years because the workload was immense. Afterward, due to health issues and the intense workload, I requested a transfer to Eskişehir. The project for Peace and Criminal Judgeships was launched in Eskişehir during that time. But I ended up being assigned as a Criminal Judge due to the government's perception of my political stance. Then the July 15 coup attempt happened. In short, that's how my life has been. I have an 18-year-long career as a judge, and since around 2016, I have been working as a lawyer, except for a 15-month period when I was in prison.

Kubra Unver: You have an impressive background, and your experiences in the field of law, particularly human rights, seem substantial. What does human rights mean to you? Sometimes people separate their personal lives from their professions, but it appears that human rights are an integral part of your life. Could you elaborate on their importance to you, both in your career and your personal life?

Kemal Karanfil: Human rights are deeply ingrained in my life, possibly influenced by family upbringing. Even when I was on the podium as a judge, I always respected human rights to the maximum extent. For instance, during my tenure as a Criminal Judge, I considered detention as a last resort. When a person was sent for arrest, I first checked if they were married and how many children they had. If they were married, I calculated the impact on their family before making any decisions. If the crime wasn't severe, I would opt for alternative penalties, such as planting trees or converting fines into community service. I even reported violations like excessive exhaust emissions from vehicles to relevant authorities. I took the same approach when I encountered potholes on the road; I reported them to ensure safety. I once even suggested to Melih Gökçek, the then-mayor of Ankara, that he should create a "Pothole Team" to monitor and repair them. In short, I approached things from a human-centric perspective. I tried to minimize the

negative impact on families and loved ones when imposing punishments. I was focused on how to help individuals become better and cause less harm to their families when applying penalties. I reported violations and worked to enhance human rights awareness. So, human rights were always at the forefront for me.

Kubra Unver: Indeed, your perspective as a judge is quite unique. You've demonstrated a remarkable attention to detail and compassion for individuals' situations. Considering the changes in your life, and the fact that you can no longer actively practice law, how do you approach these changes, and what are you currently engaged in? Could you provide us with some insights into your activities?

Kemal Karanfil: Certainly. I am a believer in life's trial process, and I will never forget that. I examine it closely. God chose me, a child from a poor family, and made me a judge, taking me to nice places, but later on, for some reason, I faced hardships. Yet, it wouldn't be right to harbor resentment and turn my back on life. That would mean criticizing the Creator. Therefore, I focus on how I can continue to be a good person in my circumstances, contribute to society, and advance human rights. After serving around 15 months in prison under ridiculous pretexts, I became involved in KHK (Decree-Law) platforms in Istanbul. I was part of the executive board of the Istanbul KHK Platform. We aimed to raise human rights awareness in various cities. When I moved abroad, I established initiatives in Europe with my friends to bring attention to human rights violations in Turkey. We sent messages to institutions, wrote letters to members of the European Court of Human Rights, organized demonstrations, and carried out various actions. I didn't stop because trials are a possibility of life. God might test humans, but humans cannot test God. A person cannot declare, "I will only be a good person in this position or under these circumstances." Every profession and every individual are valuable. A person doesn't gain value from their position; even if the judge's robe is taken away, Kemal Karanfil, as a person, will continue. If someone only gains value from their position, they will crumble when the position is taken away. KHK victims, on the other hand, are not crumbling, although they face harsh conditions. Their fundamental rights are taken away, they are excluded from private sector employment, and they are imprisoned due to lawful and routine activities. So, they face a lot of difficulties, but if their rights are not taken away, they can still make a positive impact. If their passports weren't taken away, they could have opportunities in the private sector and abroad, and they could earn five to ten times more than what they earned in Turkey.

Kubra Unver: So, it seems like you've used your profession as a tool rather than a purpose. Tools can change along the way, the paths we follow to reach our goals can change, but that doesn't mean the destination itself changes. If our destination is to serve humanity, it can be achieved through various means, including a career in law, or on different platforms, as you've demonstrated through your life experiences.

Kemal Karanfil: Thank you. I like your

observation. For example, if someone from Siirt sets out to go to Istanbul and their car breaks down, they would simply get on another bus and continue on to Istanbul. Similarly, if a person's goal is the development of their country, promoting human rights, and being a beneficial citizen, then on the journey to that goal, they may face changes in their position or be relocated elsewhere, and they shouldn't take offense. They should adjust and continue on their path by getting on another "vehicle."

💬 **Kubra Unver: Yes, sometimes we need to travel by plane, sometimes by bus, sometimes by car, sometimes by bicycle, and sometimes even by walking.**

💬 **Kemal Karanfil:** And there's also what Kubra mentioned, where you said that things people perceive as evil may actually turn out to be good. In the Quran, it's mentioned that when a vehicle breaks down, it may seem like an evil, but I've heard from many friends, especially those who go abroad, saying, "I wish I had come 40 years ago; it turns out the life we lived in Turkey couldn't even be called life."

💬 **Kubra Unver: You've ingeniously used your knowledge and expertise to champion human rights causes, and you continue to do so. What advice would you give to young people who are aspiring to contribute to human rights? Can you share a piece of advice or a tip with us?**

💬 **Kemal Karanfil:** Certainly. In many backward countries, and even in Greece, ancient philosophers used to deify the state. This perspective also existed in Turkey and Greece, where the state was considered supreme, and everything could be sacrificed for it. But the state is a creation of humans, while humans are creations of Allah. Humans are appointed as caretakers of the earth, and they are accountable to God. The Farewell Sermon of the Prophet Muhammad is one of the oldest and most beautiful universal declarations of human rights. Many modern declarations tend to overlook this, as if human rights started with the Magna Carta in 1215. However, in the Farewell Sermon, Prophet Muhammad emphasized the inviolability of property, life, and honor. Therefore, if a person truly wants to be a person and loves God, they must love all of God's creations, including humans, animals, and nature. To contribute to human rights, one should focus on these three areas and work for their well-being and peace. Why not establish an organization similar to Amnesty International by those who were expelled from Turkey or those who left the country? I believe they can do that. They should strive for it.

💬 **Kubra Unver: Indeed, your insights on the Farewell Sermon provide a fresh perspective. You've emphasized the interconnectedness of human rights, animal rights, and environmental rights. Thank you for granting us this interview, Mr. Kemal. Thank you again for your time.**

💬 **Kubra Unver:** Thank you. I wish you all the best. Have a good broadcast. 🟥

71

What was one of the main slogans of the massive protests against police brutality in the U.S. in 2020?

a) We can't party
b) We can't breathe
c) We can't eat
d) We don't like cabbage

72

The strategy developed by Mahatma Ghandi and his supporters to overthrow the British rule of India is known as?

a) Nonviolent resistance
b) Smart resistance
c) Weaponless fighting
d) Moneyless selling

73

In which year did the majority of African countries achieve independence?

a) 1945
b) 1950
c) 1957
d) 1960

74

When did King John sign the Magna Carta condition, which establishes certain rights that even the king cannot violate?

a) 915
b) 1215
c) 1800
d) 500

75

Many innocent and educated people in Turkey were arrested because they had ____ US dollar in their possession?

a) 10 thousand
b) one hundred thousand
c) thousand
d) one

76

Name the activist nun, who received the Nobel peace prize in 1979.

a) Mother Maria
b) Mother Teresa
c) Mother Joanna

77
Why was Ayse Ozdogan arrested and not released even though she has stage 4 cancer?
a) She stole the government's money.
b) She smuggled drugs with a state plane
c) She worked as an administrator in a school

78
In which event did Berkin Elvan die from getting hit by a gas canister thrown by the police at the age of 15?
a) 15 July 2016 Coup
b) 2015 Ankara Station Massacre
c) 2013 Taksim Gezi Park Protests
d) European Commission

79
How many member states does the United Nations have?
a) 58
b) 193
c) 130
d) 195

80
How many articles are in the International Bill of Human Rights also known as Basic Human Rights?
a) 10
b) 15
c) 50
d) 30

Did You Know That?

Saturday Mothers

Did you know that there is a community that comes together every week searching for those responsible for the disappearance of their detained relatives?
Saturday Mothers is a community that has been holding peaceful sit-ins in Galatasaray Square every Saturday since May 27, 1995, for almost 30 years. They come together every week with the power of their constitutional right to freedom of peaceful assembly and demonstration. Unfortunately, when the relatives of the disappeared and the lawyers who would defend them, came together for Saturday Mothers at Çağlayan courthouse for the same purpose, were attacked before the hearing and a lawsuit was filed against them. This is a wonderful

example of using your right for peaceful assembly and demonstration. It is the right to join together as a group and protest and try to raise the voices or to try to have concerns and problems heard, as they are holding the images of their lost relatives or their disappeared relatives, who they are searching for.

Gender-based violence

Did you know that 290 women were killed as a result of male violence in the first 11 months of 2021?

According to the Human Right Association and Turkey Human Rights Foundation, documentation unit data reported that 290 women were killed as a result of male violence in the first 11 months of 2021. So around 29 women were killed per month, which makes 1 woman per day. ■

Thoughts Of The Contest Winners

Selman Avci 6th Kahoot competition 2rd place

I heard about it from friends around me and participated in AST's Kahoot competition. The questions were really thought-provoking and good information was given in the conversations. I'm so glad I joined. They sent the second prize immediately. It was a very entertaining competition, both in terms of questions and topics. Thank you very much to those who did it. ■

🎙 **INTERVIEW: Our interview focused on the story behind Dr. Kari's "Unmuted" exhibition, which was organized to raise awareness about human rights violations worldwide and in Turkey.**

Mercan Kuloglu: Hello Kari!

Dr. Kari O'Rourke: Hey! Before we start I have one thing I want to do. I have $25 that I'm going to send to you, I want to add a fourth prize to your Kahoot contest.

Mercan Kuloglu: I think that's amazing, I'm sure our participants will be very excited to go fill up their survey right now for the fourth prize.

Dr. Kari O'Rourke: I will send that $25 because I want to encourage youth. And again before we get started on Un-muted, I just want to say, you probably didn't know this about me, but I have biracial children. My sons, my twin boys, are black. And they very much have experienced the driving while black experience, where the police pulled them over for no reason, and searched their cars, and kept them in handcuffs on the curb. You know, one of my sons got a ticket because his turn signals were the wrong shade of amber. That's the kind of ridiculousness that happens in racism when it's taken to the extreme. When they were in high school I worried every night. When they went out, when they were not with me, I worried and prayed for them every night. And I still do because racism is a serious problem. And what happened with George Floyd; the only reason there is any justice in the George Floyd situation is because it was caught on video.

Mercan Kuloglu: Exactly.

Dr. Kari O'Rourke: If it hadn't been caught on video they would have denied it and it would have been all George Floyd's fault. I guarantee it that's how the media would have portrayed it, and the police would have portrayed it. Yes, we have to say all lives matter, but we also have to say that that movement means black lives matter, means we need to be aware of racism and in our midst everywhere. And that's in our community and in our country, right here in the United States

Mercan Kuloglu: Exactly, exactly. And I know you're feeling a bit under the weather today, but despite that you're here with us again to stand for the victims of Turkey, victims of police brutality, and other minorities and other people who've been oppressed. So I want to talk about today; I know you do so much and I love you for that, but I want to talk about the Un-muted exhibition that you had here in Kansas City. So just one, there's a million questions I think I can ask about that, but one that really interests me is why did you call it Un-muted?

Dr. Kari O'Rourke: Well because I really, you know, Advocates of Silence Turkey, I don't think the victims in Turkey have been silenced. Now certainly, the people who have died are silent, they're not able to speak on their own behalf. But I don't think those voices are silent. I think those voices are screaming for justice, they're yelling to get out and it's loud. And they're clamoring lots of great adjectives to describe how loud those voices are. And I think it's our responsibility to listen to those voices. And so, you know, just like in this thing there's a little mute button down here on the screen, and that's a word that we all are accustomed to. I think we need to Un-mute, so that we can hear what's happening there. And as soon as we hear what's happening there, then we're compelled to do something. We can't just stand by and do nothing. That's how I came up with that anyway, it was random, but it seemed like it fit to me.

Mercan Kuloglu: I definitely love that because we don't think about it, we use the word silent so easily. But yeah you're totally right, because they're not actually silenced, they're screaming, you know, in their own ways. There are Twitter posts or their families asking for prayers, they're screaming to have their voices heard. And I think unmuted is such a wonderful word to use too because, you know, they're there. We just have to raise that voice up, raise the volume bar up for them. So thank you so much.

Dr. Kari O'Rourke: Just a little grammar note, at the very end of my presentation, during the when I did the Un-muted presentations. Instead of calling it Un-muted, in the past tense, I put it Un-mute, in the verb tense to say "Go do this". Now is our job to go and unmute that voice and to say something

Mercan Kuloglu: Hopefully that's what we're trying to do here, in Advocates of Silenced Turkey, there are many events and, you know, this kahoot competition too, we're trying to unmute these voices through very different and creative methods. So another

question is, what is one item from the exhibition that truly affected you?

💬 **Dr. Kari O'Rourke:** The first item that truly affected me was again kind of random, and it was when we were in New Jersey together. So it was before we brought the exhibit to Kansas City. I was standing there just kind of trying to familiarize myself, I just arrived and was trying to familiarize myself with everything, and kind of looking at things, and thinking 'Wow this is really big' you know, and a woman came up to me who didn't speak English very well, but she came up and she saw me looking at this artifact. It was a frame with a jacket in it, and she said that was my brother's. I was like 'Oh my goodness! What, are you kidding me, wow!' What do you say to this woman, you know, I'm like 'Oh, I'm so sorry, but I'm so grateful that you're here and it's here', you know. And then the next thing that happened is, you know, then we had our event, it was great, and we planned to bring it to Kansas City, and it took a lot of logistics and whatever. And the artifacts arrived on the truck, and the guy called me at the last minute and said "Hey, I'm here. I got your truck, I'm here." And I'm like, "You know you were supposed to call me ahead of time", and he's like "Oh no, well I'm here now." And so I had to get dressed really fast and run down to the church and get somebody to come help. And you helped me find somebody, they came to help, and they didn't speak English very much, but he's a wonderful man, he's from Turkey. And he helped me unload the heavy items because they brought it on these big pallets and stuff, and it wouldn't fit through the door, you know. So I had to unload everything and take it in, and I was taking it in and there were about 10 boxes left on the palette, and it was kind of heavy and so when he arrived, he carried the heavy stuff in. And the very last box he picked up off the bottom of the pallet, he picked up and he started to carry it in, and then his whole face changed, his whole demeanor changed. And you know like on the outside of the boxes, the names were just kind of written in big magic markers, scribbled on there, you know. He said "I knew this man. I worked with this man in Azerbaijan." and I was like "Are you kidding me, wow." He goes "Yeah, yeah." And what I could really sense from him was, in Christianity, well in Irish Christianity anyway, in Irish folklore we have this saying called "There but for the grace of God go I" And it means, you know, somehow it could have been anyone that was in that box, instead it was this other guy, you know. "There but for the grace of God go I". And he was having that moment. I will tell you, that man came to every event, every time I needed a volunteer to help, that man showed up. So I know this was deeply personal for him.

💬 **Mercan Kuloglu: Yeah, definitely. And that's one of many possibly who are in that exhibition who, you know, the names weren't so strange, they were actually pretty familiar to them. So another question is, that I kind of asked you this in our first program too, but you know, there's so much going on, why Turkey, why should we care about Turkey and what's happening there?**

💬 **Dr. Kari O'Rourke:** Right, and you know what I always say because you have a privilege to that, but first of all, as we started this

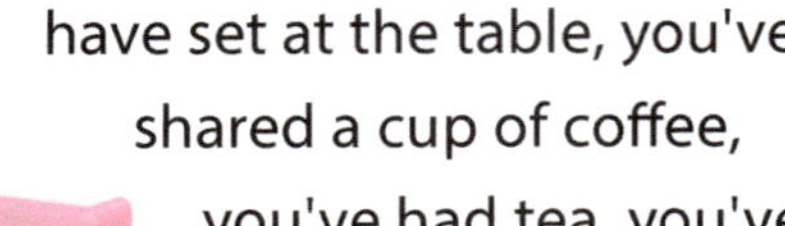

program, in my own community, here in Kansas City, we have a lot of problems, we have a lot of gun violence, and I think that's probably true in New Jersey and other parts of the country. The United States and in the world, you know, every community has its own issues, right: poverty, hunger, we're having gun violence right now, racism. In our country we have a lot of issues going on, I mean we have, again, racism and George Floyd and the Black lives matter movement. And you know it's huge, right and then we have the country, we have the world, we have this global vision. We can't be so myopic that we only worry about ourselves. We have to think about the bigger picture. And the reason I'm connected with Advocates of Silenced Turkey is because I met people who are from Turkey, I met people who have crossed the river to get here and, you know, I have my coffee cup right, and the Turkish proverb is - a single cup of coffee unites us for 40 years. And I always say, be careful who you have coffee with, we'll be best friends forever, right. 40 years is a lifetime and I had coffee with you Mercan, so we are united for a lifetime. But the truth of the matter is once you are so intimate with somebody, that you

have set at the table, you've shared a cup of coffee, you've had tea, you've had some baklava, you've had a cookie, a biscuit or whatever, you know, had a meal together, it becomes deeply personal. And then when I have to put my arms around someone who's crying, because they're viewing this exhibit in Kansas City. They had the privilege, it was a privilege for that exhibit to come here, it was a tremendous privilege because the Turkish community in Kansas City weren't able to come to New Jersey, right. So it helped heal the wounds of the people who were living, the Turkish community here in Kansas City that grieves for their loss. But also, the bigger picture was, it brought awareness to the Christian community. To the community who could provide support right here in Kansas City to our Turkish brothers and sisters. And it bridged, that's the whole idea is, it bridged. What we really showed is how this is a very sacred journey, a very sacred, very delicate, you know, so fragile, these lives that we were touching. So many people wept tears, sincere tears. We had lots of tissue boxes because people really were moved. And so we had this three nights, as you know, and it was sacred, that's the only way, you know. And

A DISSERTATION ABOUT SOCIAL GENOCIDE OF HIZMET MOVEMENT

TURKIC EDUCATORS AND STUDENTS BREAKING THEIR SILENCE:

AN ORAL HISTORY OF A TANGLED WEB OF POLITICAL POWER

A DISSERTATION IN

Educational Leadership, Policy, and Foundations
and Curriculum and Instruction

Presented to the Faculty of the University
of Missouri-Kansas City in partial fulfillment of
the requirements for the degree

DOCTOR OF PHILOSOPHY

By

Kari L. O'Rourke

B.A., Saint Mary College, 1985

M.B.A., University of Missouri-Kansas City, 1998

Kansas City, Missouri
2023

it's only through the grace of God bringing everything together to make this happen, because it took so much effort from so many people. I was just a pawn in the big game, you know, of getting this. It took people getting the artifacts to New Jersey, it took Aslahan and Humeyra and all the others in New Jersey and Aysegul. All the people, it took all those people putting that together. It's a lot of money. It was not cheap to ship all that stuff here, you know. It took a lot for all that to happen. And it seems very clear to me that it was the will of God, it was the will of Allah that this happened. That we bring this together and make this happen because there's no way it could have happened otherwise.

Mercan Kuloglu: Definitely. Well thank you! I mean my one final question before we close this off is, where do you think this exhibition will go to? I don't mean physically, like from another state, but I mean what doors will it open in the future?

Dr. Kari O'Rourke: Well, I can tell you this, the point of the whole thing is to give hope to people who right now feel very hopeless. When people are down as far as they can get, you know, this is going to help lift them up. And I've asked people to write letters. And one connection we make is I teach this class online to my Turkish friends, English language class, you know. And we were looking at the pictures, and Ali saw a picture and he said "Back up, back up, I want to see that picture", and he goes, "I know that man, that man is here with me in Germany", in a refugee apartment or a complex, right. And we're going to send letters to him to let him know that we care. We already sent him a picture of his part of the exhibit. He lost his wife and three children, crossing the river they drowned. We've already sent him a photo of his family being honored in this presentation. How does that make him feel? That's going to make him feel very like, wow, you know, like he is feeling that blessing of wow, somebody cares. That's what we're here to do, is to let people know we care. So there are several college students that are going to write to him, and I will get the letters to him. We're going to write letters to people who are in prison and let them know 'Hey, don't give up, hang in there, we know it stinks, this is not much fun, but hang in there, we're going to be with you.'

Mercan Kuloglu: Definitely. Our prayers are what matters, you know, our actions to help them out, remind them that they're not alone, that their stories aren't going to go, you know, buried away, it's going to be with us, continuing. So thank you so much, first of all for this Un-muted Social Genocide Exhibition. I think it's monumental and I hope it goes to places that we've never even thought it could. And I hope it raises, unmutes their voices in a way that we didn't think was possible maybe. But first of all thank you for that, and then thank you for coming here today despite feeling a little sick. Yeah I hope in the future, you know, programs, this is our second program together.

Dr. Kari O'Rourke: This is our second one and I'm telling you, this Un-muted exhibit is going to go around the country, it may even go to another country, maybe go elsewhere. But this is just the first of many, and you know once that momentum, it's the ripple effect that creates this tsunami. And a tsunami of love and care and concern is really what's going to happen, it's going to flow out of this, I believe that.

Mercan Kuloglu: Definitely, thank you so much for joining us today Kari!

Dr. Kari O'Rourke: Sure!

81

The Universal Declaration of Human Rights was most recently translated into which language?
a) French
b) Welsh
c) Arabic
d) Urdu

82

In his decision in the Yüksel Yalçınkaya v. Turkey Case dated 26 September 2023, he made very important findings and evaluations regarding the trials carried out in Turkey after 15 July 2016, especially on the allegation of being a member of the Gülen Movement, and ultimately concluded Article 6 of the European Convention on Human Rights (ECHR), which regulates the right to a fair trial. Which court decided that Article 7, which regulates the principle that there will be no crime without law, and Article 11, which relates to the right to organize and assemble, were violated?
a) Supreme Court
b) European Court of Human Rights
c) Constitutional Court
d) Court of Justice of the European Union

83

Entrepreneur detained for 4.5 years, awaiting his release after the decision by the ECHR that his detention is unlawful.
a) Osman Kavala
b) Selahattin Demirtas
c) Omer Gergerlioglu

84

Which of the following is NOT a crime for Uyghurs in China?
a) Speaking Uyghur
b) Reading a book in the Uyghur language
c) Having traditional Uyghur carpets
d) Calling yourself 'Chinese'

8 5 The public movement fighting for granting women the right to vote in America was called?
a) Feminists
b) Abolitionists
c) Anti-sexists
d) Suffragists

8 6 Who was an English writer and advocate of women rights and philosopher?
a) Harriet Tubman
b) Susan B. Anthony
c) Mary Wollstonecraft

8 7 Who is the Kurdish politician whose body was sent to her family in Diyarbakır by cargo after she was tortured to death?
a) Garibe Gezer
b) Spring Wolf
c) Helin Borek

8 8 Mandela is a South African anti-discrimination activist and the first black president of the Republic of South Africa.
a) True
b) False

8 9 According to the OSHA at least 1853 people died in the first 10 months of 2021 in Turkey as a result of?
a) Traffic accident
b) Heart attacks
c) Workplace accidents
d) Natural disasters

9 0 Which democracy principle is related to the coexistence of different ideas and the ability to express thoughts?
a) Constitutionalism
b) Equality
c) Pluralism
d) National Sovereignty

Did You Know That?

Poor working conditions in Turkey

Did you know that 1853 workers lost their lives in the first 10 months of 2021?
According to the occupational health and safety board data, 1853 people lost their lives as a result of work accident/murder in the first 10 months of 2021 in Turkey because of poor working conditions. ■

🎤 INTERVIEW: "Our interview with Dr. Yucel discussing human rights violations and our work at AST."

💬 **Mercan Kuloglu:** Today, a very important guest will be connected. He is assistant professor Dr. Dogan Yucel. Lecturer, linguist, writer, educator and literary scholar. He also works at International Burç University and today he will connect from Europe and tell us a little bit about human rights studies. Welcome Doctor Yucel. How are you?

💬 **Dr. Dogan Yucel:** Thank you. How are you?

💬 **Mercan Kuloglu:** I'm fine too, thank goodness. Now I have a few questions for you. First, can you tell us a little about your education and job?

💬 **Dr. Dogan Yucel:** Yes, I am currently taking master's and doctoral courses. I teach linguistics. Department of Turkish Language and Literature. At the same time, Turkish lessons are still continuing at a college.

💬 **Mercan Kuloglu:** Great, but I think your work has a connection with human rights. How do you use this for human rights and what have you done so far?

💬 **Dr. Dogan Yucel:** Of course, people have free time, everyone has something they can do. We are creatures that exist with human emotions. An entity seeking freedom, rights and law. Everyone has, more or less, injustices and unlawfulness they experience in this world, and they have to struggle with them as well. There is a very famous saying, "not only for himself, that he who helps you today and me tomorrow, who helps those who can't afford it when he has the opportunity, will also get help tomorrow when he doesn't have the opportunity." With that thought in mind, everyone should do something they can do with their hands, voice, and heart. We must stand by what's right and the law.

🗨 Mercan Kuloglu: Yes, you are very right. Indeed, while we have the opportunities right now, while we can encourage people, especially our young people who do not understand the unlawfulnesses, we can explain these situations, while we can raise them to help others, we definitely need to use our opportunities with today's or other methods. Well, can you tell us a little bit about your experience at AST?

🗨 Dr. Dogan Yucel: So, we had some acquaintances at AST. Somehow later on they reached us. Maybe those who watched here remember last year, there were stories of hope that I edited. Then my daughter participated in the painting competition, she came in first place. After that, I gave different help, that is information to the best of my knowledge and experiences. Also, as a family we won the last competition.

🗨 Mercan Kuloglu: Will we see your children in the first and second ones today?

🗨 Dr. Dogan Yucel: Let's see, I won't help, so there is no cheating. I'm not going to help while I'm here, but let's see if they can do it without their father.

🗨 Mercan Kuloglu: I hope so. So what are your recommendations for the efforts to defend the human rights of the audience? I know that there are many young people among us who are younger than me, so I couldn't believe it. Well, for us, can you share your thoughts on how we can defend human rights, how we can become activists?

🗨 Dr. Dogan Yucel: When I was little, about eight years old, my grandfather passed away. I compared my age with my grandfather's age in my head. My grandfather was 62 when he passed away, it seemed too long, so how can a person live to be 62 years old. Now, when we start to approach those ages, when I look back, life seems to pass like a second, so these people, our younger siblings, may think that they had a lot longer in their lives, but life is really very short. One way or another, it will pass very quickly, and when they look back on their lives, they should pay attention to what they have done and what traces they have left. In other words, did they leave something that was beneficial to useful people, or did they only think of their own value and spent a life that was not beneficial to anyone, they should look at it, they should pay attention to this. Life really goes by very fast for those who do good deeds among good and bad ones and those who do harmful things to people.

🗨 Mercan Kuloglu: You are very right, sir, then what we will understand here is that you should act now, because as you said, life will pass by saying that tomorrow will be after this exam, after this project. It's like for a second. For a second, you are saying that we need to act now, so I agree very much, and in the same way, I try to adjust my day according to it, I try to live according to it, my Lord, I hope it will be successful for all of us. Thank you very much for connecting. 

91 Which modern thinker laid the foundations for today's liberal understanding of human rights?
a) Thomas Hobbes
b) Jean Bodin
c) John Locke
d) Montesquieu

93 Which of the following is not a characteristic of human rights?
a) Human rights only apply in developed countries
b) These are the traits we are born with.
c) These are inviolable and inalienable rights.
d) Human rights are not given, they are recognized

95 What is the name given to the violence and human rights violations against the Uyghurs by the Chinese Communist Party?
a) Chinese civil war
b) Chino-Uyghur war
c) Uyghur genocide
d) None of the above
d) Human rights are not given, they are recognized

92 What is the name of the Swedish activist who became famous for her 'How dare you!' speech at the 2019 UN Climate Summit?
a) Beta Ulberg
b) Agatha Nurenberg
c) Arigatto Gatorade
d) Greta Thunberg

94 What is the name of the font that detained journalist Fevzi Yazıcı, former visual director of Zaman newspaper, designed in prison?
a) Ferdowsi
b) Helvetica
c) Verdena
d) Kuseyri

96 What is the name of the ex-military student, whose last goodbye to his mother was painted by the artist and activist, Gianluca Costantini?
a) Fatih Tailor
b) Ali Osman Kavak
c) Ahmet Yasar
d) Mustafa Enis Durak

97

Who is the African-American man who was killed by a police officer while being detained on suspicion of fraud in the US?
a) George Floyd
b) Michael Floyd
c) George Foreman
d) Michael Foreman

98

Which situation below is related to the problems concerning freedom of expression in Turkey?
a) Censorship imposed on journalists
b) Police intervention in peaceful demonstrations
c) Closure of civil society organizations
d) All of the above

99

Which factors contribute to the increase in human rights violations in Turkey?
a) Fighting terrorism
b) Expansion of government powers
c) Limited press freedom
d) All of the above

100

What is the most common area of violation of the right to a fair trial in Turkey?
a) Arrests within the scope of combating terrorism
b) Legal processes against political dissidents
c) Detention and arrests of government opponents
d) All of the above

Thoughts Of The Contest Winners

Doğan Yüceloğlu 7th Kahoot Competition 3rd

Hello. First of all, I find it very valuable that such an organization has been organized. AST's Kahoot competition is perhaps one of the firsts. As a family, we tried to participate in almost all competitions, whether we received an award or not. This contest brought excitement to us. Not only did we narrowly miss places, but we also finished in the top three a few times. We got some questions we knew wrong and some we didn't know right :)

I wanted to prepare for the last competition as a volunteer. I even attended as a speaker. I learned many things about human rights that I did not know before. At least I had the opportunity to hear about important works in painting, literature and other branches of art. I believe that it is a duty of humanity to always participate in AST's competitions, such as the Kahoot competition or its other activities, and to support them through these activities. Thank you.

🔑 ANSWER KEY

#	Ans	#	Ans	#	Ans	#	Ans	#	Ans
1	a	25	c	49	d	73	d	97	a
2	c	26	b	50	c	74	b	98	d
3	a	27	a	51	d	75	d	99	d
4	c	28	c	52	a	76	b	100	d
5	c	29	b	53	b	77	c		
6	b	30	a	54	d	78	c		
7	c	31	c	55	c	79	b		
8	c	32	c	56	b	80	d		
9	b	33	c	57	b	81	b		
10	b	34	d	58	d	82	b		
11	d	35	b	59	a	83	a		
12	c	36	a	60	c	84	d		
13	a	37	c	61	a	85	d		
14	b	38	c	62	d	86	c		
15	d	39	a	63	c	87	a		
16	c	40	b	64	c	88	a		
17	d	41	c	65	b	89	c		
18	c	42	a	66	c	90	c		
19	b	43	c	67	b	91	c		
20	a	44	b	68	c	92	d		
21	b	45	d	69	a	93	a		
22	b	46	d	70	a	94	a		
23	a	47	c	71	b	95	c		
24	d	48	c	72	a	96	d